FITZPATRICK

FITZPATRICK

Richard Carr

Broadstone

Library of Congress Control Number 2017959960

ISBN 978-1-937968-40-3

Design & Typesetting by Larry W. Moore

Cover artwork used by permission

Broadstone Books
An Imprint of
Broadstone Media LLC
418 Ann Street
Frankfort, KY 40601-1929
BroadstoneBooks.com

CONTENTS

HIS BARTENDER

THE BASTARD

His Wife

The Work

HIS BARTENDER

1.

Fitzpatrick's belly was an iron tank
capable of containing anything—all the beer and whiskey in
       the bar,
wagonloads of potatoes and steak.

His wire glasses were like gauges on a steam engine,
needles hovering dangerously over incomprehensible numbers.
Interrupted, he'd blink hard,

and his real eyes would show through—blue of evening sky
with clouds rolling in.
Outwardly genial,

he ate like a machine.
Something in his hot core troubled him, some indigestion
       maybe,
but he was too large to be stopped.

2.

Those days you could smoke,
and Fitzpatrick smoked while he smoked,
one hand raising and lowering a cigarette,
the other fondling the red pack.

Sometimes he left the cigarette in his mouth,
dangling helplessly, like a cartoon coyote on a cliff,
and used the freed hand to scribble on a pad,
the pen burning in his fingers.

Sometimes the other hand left the pack on the bar
and rose to his face, not to help any damned coyote,
but to touch his twitching cheek with a question,
eyelids fanning the smoke.

The black ashtray a pit
filled with amber bones,
question marks ran down his cheeks like tears.
The smoke never cleared.

3.

He wore a thick mask,
pocked, stubbled,

heavy browed.
The brows were two continents crushed against each other.

The eyeholes
peepholes.

He looked
up from his beer to the mirror and quickly down.

He eavesdropped on conversations.
He offended my customers

or frightened them when he suddenly pulled off the mask
to correct some point of fact.

People saw the bare bones of his face,
muscle and sinew,

and turned away, made a wall of their backs
to guard the little flame of their friendship.

Fitzpatrick straightened his shoulders,
glancing sideways through the holes in his mask.

4.

He had a bar friend, another bastard
or schoolboy who penciled in the margins
his gritting mockery of the dance crowd,

unloaded piles of derisive bricks on the young pool players,
and marauded the college kids in their hamlets among the
        booths
for their beauty and stupidity.

With his thin smile, Fitzpatrick approved the cruel mirth,
commanded it,
and when he muttered to his friend, both showed their teeth
        in famished grins.

Together they were like wolves sharing a kill,
though not sharing equally: The bastard pawed the carcass
while Fitzpatrick ate.

5.

His wife rarely drank with him,
though she drank—
short whiskeys which she hid with her hand
or protected from encroachment.

She drank like a card player,
nodded for another.
Sitting next to Fitzpatrick in suspicious silence,
she waited for his answer.

Fitzpatrick always pushed back his barstool in her presence
and put one foot on the floor
like a gentleman.
Baronial, he paid her tab.

She shook her red hair on her way to the door.
Sometimes she looked back.
Always he watched her go
in the mirror.

6.

Returning to his thoughts,
Fitzpatrick tapped the bar with his middle finger.

He always seemed to be counting something.
His lips moved.

He blinked rhythmically
or stared so blankly I thought he'd fall asleep.

Then the tapping would resume,
like a pianist playing one graceful note—stuck on it.

I think he was looking for the next note, the next thought,
poking about in a box of old photos

or tripping through some endless file system.
Eventually he'd find something,

his mouth opening into a small "o"
while he thought about it

and began tapping the new note.

7.

Fitzpatrick understood the bar business.
He frowned over money
but kept little shrines of it in his pockets.

He could be affable.
He talked about cars, motorcycles, and Michelangelo
charmingly, like a bubbling stream.

In the mood, he was good for business.
Customers asked after him, like an old uncle
or the memory of a childhood sideshow.

Even at his foulest,
when he grumbled drunkenly into his drink,
or derided everyone as fools for watching the local news,

I admired him.
He was an old house
which had stood longer than its lords.

8.

Built like a goat,
the bastard braced his arms against the bar,
craned his neck downward to drink.

He laughed like a goat,
coughing,
and he had the dead, inscrutable glare of a goat.

It was always imported beer in a pint glass
for him, his deep trough,
and a moustache hair in the dregs.

Goat-gray, his scratched face stretched
and sagged, stretched and sagged,
calculating

a tip.
He chewed on each tip like a goat gnawing rope
until a small remainder fell from his mouth.

9.

Fitzpatrick's wife came to the bar alone one day
to ask questions.

She looked through me like a cop, asked cop questions
about the fugitive.

I told her what I told every cop and wife: He was here,
he drank, he left.

If there were other women, she asked with every gesture...
But that was not for me to say.

Then she spoke of him in the past tense. Gravely I said
he'll come home.

10.

I work on my feet, like any streetwalker
or stage actor.
I stand, like any goddamned hotdog vendor,
until I am wanted.

I stand at ease,
twisting a white bar towel behind my back.
I look over the heads of the drinkers
like some stolid sentry.

A watchman on the castle wall,
I scan the cocktail tables without interest or authority.
Candles, little fires burning all night,
light the encampment.

Sometimes I don't remember making drinks
or taking money.
But always, Fitzpatrick setting his empty glass on the bar
shattered me.

11.

Every time I broke a glass,
Fitzpatrick leaned over the bar to see the shards.

Though huge, like a horse, or a president,
he backed away from a drop of blood.

I thought I understood him,
presuming his physical strength a necessity of some inner
          weakness.

I hated that I could not see into his brain.
Never his friend,

I measured his big shoulders against mine
and found us equal.

It was a lie, and it chilled me to know it.
Fitzpatrick burned silently like a nuclear reactor,

and I could never see the atoms of him,
the bright, clashing energy

which he controlled
and fed.

Benign, he offered to help,
and I brushed his kindness into the trash.

12.

His bastard friend laughed tunelessly
like a lawyer.
Fitzpatrick's attention swiveled to him.

They lifted their eyes toward women
and spoke quietly,
adversaries admiring each other's clients.

Occasionally they bought drinks for men
to make a better joke of them,
a game for the bastard, a gambit for Fitzpatrick.

Eventually the bastard smoothed his tie and paid his tab,
laughing tirelessly.
Fitzpatrick closed up like a file drawer

and sat silently while his friend said good-bye.

13.

In time his wife stopped asking about him,
though she came for drinks more often.

She looked around the bar like a tourist,
smiled like she didn't know me.

Fitzpatrick ignored her pretty remarks
like wind ruffling his hair.

She produced newspaper clippings
which he swatted away with the back of his hand,

bothered by the buzz of the flies
but happier and quieter than before.

He shrugged away her touch
and closed his eyes, solemn as a cat.

As always, she stiffened and left early,
turning at the door to check her watch.

14.

Fitzpatrick's tweedy manner suggested money.
That he came from, made, or married it
many presumed.
He never explained his stature, and so it grew.

I thought he lived on wages and windfall
like any wannabe in the city
except the decades did not erode him to gravel
but cut him smooth features.

Pigeons sat on him.
His bearing invited picnickers and school busses.
His polished surfaces attracted artists and bankers.
By closing time, he was poor and dirty.

15.

One night we stayed late to enjoy the quiet.
I shared his cigarette.
We watched the busboy mop the floor.

Fitzpatrick had drunk too much,
and a pale blue flame roamed his body,
consuming the last of his output.

I wiped down the bar,
and Fitzpatrick lifted his elbows.
I helped him on with his coat

and walked him home,
his arm still hot
when I left him at the top of his stairs.

THE BASTARD

1.

We buttoned up our shirts and squared our shoulders,
laughed inwardly like talent agents
or priests
at the weaknesses of others.

Fitzpatrick lit my cigarette.
I raised my glass.
To good days
we drank, tossing the football of our good fortune.

And to bad days we drank,
slouched like bears.
With our great hairy arms we pounded the bar
to bring on the unseen enemy.

Like friends, we stood in salute, and admiration,
and drank,
and burst out laughing like talk-show hosts
at the misfortunes of others.

2.

Fitzpatrick was his own highest authority,
invincible in debate,
godlike, flawed, no friend of Man,
a shadow in the lives of those who loved him,
the silence of our sleep.

I played along.
To me he was Rome in ruins,
beautiful and dead.
For him I was the barbarian who lived among the stones
and fragments of his art.

I was the naked crazy
Other.
He called me the stick-man,
gave me the same gray as the street, a smudge
trying to catch a cab.

3.

Fitzpatrick was like snow in the city, glittering as it falls,
winking at the girls.

He arrived at the bar in good spirits
and shook the snow from his topcoat like a matador.

If he painted something during the day—
he would not say what,

as though his conquistadors had sailed
secretly—

but if he painted, he was happy.
He ate and smoked, warm as a wood stove.

Slush dripped from his shoes
into black pools.

He tensed when someone opened the door
and let in a snake of wind.

Time and whiskey softened him, and he slipped into
thought,
sat, a dark snowbank splashed by trucks.

4.

Sprung from his sleepy reverie like a startled dog,
Fitzpatrick yelped my name.

He pronounced me a corporate whore,
growling the last rolling R.

I swirled my drink
to remind him of my standard reply.

He despised my constructs
as phalluses.

I sipped.
I have money.

5.

Irish on his mother's side,
even more Irish on his father's side,
Fitzpatrick had a lively mind and a moody patriotism.

Great great grandson of forgotten immigrants,
he had a good memory
for a grudge.

He savored his enemies and rebuked his friends.
He drank whiskey like a common man
but squinted and shivered,

and I couldn't help cheering him on.

6.

Fitzpatrick mentioned his wife
in the same way he noted pedestrians passing the window—
in undertones.

Crooked nose, lovely elbows, long stride.

She carried a dead weight on one shoulder.
The other pointed upward in a shrug.
She was a witch, of course.

Crooked nose, lovely elbows, long stride.

Her words flew out singed around the edges.
The more she smiled, the hotter the words burned.
Fitzpatrick saw only her idiosyncrasies and trivialities.

Crooked nose, lovely elbows, long stride.

She would not speak to me without showing her teeth,
and I showed her mine.
Fitzpatrick looked out the window and murmured in his drink.

7.

His wife turned him into a pig.
He stank.
His cologne smelled like wet sawdust
and the cold sweat of prison.

He liked to remind her of his independence
by playing the boor
to her windswept majesty.
He farted.

When she straightened his lapels,
his jaw hung
like a little retard at the playground.
She smiled.

For him she had a kind smile,
womanly.
He kissed her cheek and held her chair
and whispered in her ear.

8.

I once shared a cab with Fitzpatrick's wife,
followed her out of the bar, skipping to catch up,

just drunk enough
to bluster some pretense of going her way.

She shuffled across the back seat without acknowledgment.
Like a bum on a bus, I settled down close to her

and waited for the cab to lurch into traffic
to seal her commitment to me.

Her chemistry changed,
releasing a purple blossom of fragrance.

Deep jasmine darkened the car.
I spoke of my projects,

accustomed to speaking of my projects,
summarizing, selling,

comfortable and fluent in my own language
and business always a pleasure

and a risk—
Jasmine brave,

my eyes groped hers
dizzily.

She turned to her window and opened it
to clear the air,

and I got out in a strange neighborhood.

9.

I stood in quaking defiance
of Fitzpatrick's talent.
I would have punched him in the face
if I'd thought it would change his expression.

He wore the stupid serenity of a transit cop
watching commuters come and go.
Like the red brick train shed echoing with afternoon traffic,
his mind filled with shafts of light.

He tapped his cigarette
and forgot our conversation.
I waited,
like a kid at the zoo waiting for the tortoise to move.

All my thoughts had price stickers on the bottom
like the snow globes and statuettes in the souvenir kiosk.
I could imagine bigger domes and greater monuments.
I could think in the millions.

Fitzpatrick walked along the platform without me.
Furious,
I strode after him, my coat flying.
Steel wheels rang in the vast space between us.

10.

He carried the ball for the underdogs
in a natural turf championship
loss.

Men pounded their chests in salute.
The young Fitzpatrick posed like a trophy—
and shimmered into oblivion.

Mysterious decades passed
before his first crude paintings emerged,
like mushrooms.

When I knew him, he still played like he could win,
and his work hung in galleries,
and all his faces shimmered.

11.

I invented Fitzpatrick's infidelity
to drive away his wife.

She confronted me in the men's room.
I looked up

and saw the craquelure of her face in the mirror.
The crazy bitch

disbelieved and blamed me both.
I told her it was all in the past—

almost all—
confiding like a friend.

She whirled against the door like a car wreck.
I held her up by the elbows

and raised my eyebrows honestly.

12.

His wife staged the opera of his public life.
It could only end badly,
as opera must.

She buried him preemptively
and hyped the tragedy,
controlling ticket sales exclusively.

She arranged his interviews
and answered all the questions,
mourning him prematurely.

She accepted dinner invitations
and attended on the arm of his effigy.
She maneuvered him.

Meanwhile, I had a quiet drink with Fitzpatrick.
He thought more, spoke less,
tapped the ice cube floating in his glass.

She threw a shroud over him.

13.

The bartender turned his back on me,
tolerated my presence
like one tolerates middle age baldness
or morning breath.

He thought of me as a mere beer drinker,
or worse,
a low grade nuisance, a dog in the alley,
or a bum with a few bucks.

But I was a bastard with good money.
I tugged on each shirt cuff,
clopped a black hoof against the floor,
and the bartender turned round.

He slid a foaming beer slowly down the bar,
like pushing a boy on a bicycle,
and let it go—with a wink to let me know
I was alone.

14.

I missed Fitzpatrick's cruelty.
Without him to set my trajectory,
I was a knife flung clumsily.

The bar filled and emptied
while I sat.
The city slept and woke.

Holidays chimed and fell to ashes.
I ate and drank alone,
lashed out halfheartedly,

like a sick cat.
My few words erupted like vomit,
which I swallowed forcefully.

15.

My mouth tasted like garbage
when I met Fitzpatrick on the street.

I watched him peel back a candy bar wrapper
and take a tentative bite.

He had become primitive.
His shoulders sloped forward under his coat collar.

Round nocturnal eyes observed me innocently
while he chewed.

Was this my friend?
He slapped my shoulder and walked on.

HIS WIFE

1.

I married Fitzpatrick for his mind:
brick and glass cosmopolitan,
boyish in meditation,
naked as a horse.

I understood the whip and leather of law,
the calculus of white-water rapids,
the economics of my adventures,
and approached him at the bar.

A statue of a horse,
he stood with his head thrown back.
My words circled him like pigeons,
and a few alit.

2.

Fitzpatrick was loved at the bar
like a knockoff handbag.

He was handed around and admired
and left at the coat rack.

I loved him in the unattended moments
in the shadows of the cloak room.

We rubbed shoulders with furs and cashmeres,
kissed with open eyes stung by smoke.

He held a drink in his big hand,
held me in his other arm.

I couldn't help smiling at him.
He was the real thing.

3.

He ate out, he said, to think alone
in a crowd.
When I arrived and pressed myself against him,

he pressed back with his elbow
and gazed at his plate.
I backed away from the gesture,

choked with the violence of it
for days.
He grew brighter and began new work,

paintings filled with windows of light
and open doors.
There was a whiteness I could not see through,

and when I asked him for one word about it
all doors closed
and the windows were shattered with blackness and lightning.

4.

He needed to work to be happy.
If he painted, he came to bed hungry.
I fed him the morsels of my body.

Other nights he lay asleep growling,
television flickering on his eyelids.
In the kitchen, I pondered the refrigerator.

5.

His primitive personality was half his genius.
He gratified himself
for anyone to see.

In the studio, he kept busy.
His eyes roved everywhere
but widened, hardened into focus on the canvas.

In a gallery, he roamed
with a big question hanging from his jaw.
His look drew people to him.

They wrote checks.
He shook hands
and ducked out for a drink.

In the bar he was received like a hero,
as though he'd saved the place from burning down.
He clasped his hands above his head.

6.

His drinking friend, a superb bastard,
waited for him like a dog at the fence.
He trotted with his master,
chin up, superior to all other pedestrians.

Fitzpatrick was no pedestrian.
He hailed a cab not by waving
but pointing at it.
The car stopped, and the two bastards climbed in.

At the bar they were like roughhousing children,
at odds, alike,
stomping proudly through the playground—
bad children.

I had to stop them.
Their conversations were repetitive and tedious,
like the jokes of old men
and the alibis of felons—not worth hearing.

At closing time the lights went up.
At home I waited like a magistrate,
delivered my long-considered judgment, without crying,
and put out the lights.

7.

His thoughts grew on his face like tufts of moss
which shriveled and fell away.
Runic figures were scratched in the stone of his cheeks,
but who could read them?

He sat in a wooden chair and looked out the back window
at the brick of the next building.
Debris rose on dusty drafts in the alley canyon,
and his eyes followed it upward,

then searched downward for the source—or fell closed,
which was the same to me.
He was a pyramid, and in some tiny, deep chamber
a pharaoh folded himself for sleep.

8.

Anniversaries passed like winter solstice,
observed quietly.

His bastard friend, a better looking man,
sent flowers.

They were red roses of condolence,
I suppose.

There was never a card.
The courier was hostile and mute.

As the snow flew, the petals crinkled and fell.
Fitzpatrick

sat sideways at the breakfast table
to ignore them.

His journeys to the bar approached a springtime
in someone else's arms,

and I clung to him all the more
for the last of his warmth.

9.

He read reviews secretly
on a bench at the train station,
his overcoat spilling around him like a waterfall.

In my office downtown I made a scrapbook,
prolonging a nubile fascination
behind closed doors.

I felt his dread.
My collages of clippings and snapshots aged like skin.
Spots formed.

Wrinkles could not be smoothed.
Death could not be abstracted.
The critics called to him in their thin voices.

10.

The bartender underwrote Fitzpatrick's reputation
with swift service
and the gravitas of nodding silence

but could not prop up the old man's head,
as I could, cupping his cheeks in my hands
to amplify his thoughts.

The bartender nodded.
Our circle of followers nodded
when I spoke.

Fitzpatrick lifted his shoulders with effort,
neither confirming nor denying
what I felt in my heart.

11.

One day running late for work
I locked him in his studio.
I was worried.

A bird in a cage, he bruised his arm against the door,
not badly.
Otherwise he flew about as usual.

When I called him to dinner that evening
he flung brushes and jars at me
without full conviction.

Afterwards he locked the door from inside,
grew jittery, deliberate,
and gulag thin.

I brought him glossy magazines and cigarettes.
He reclined, crossed his legs
and posed like a movie star gone cold

for no one to see.
I managed his revival
with only stick figures and scrawls.

12.

He flirted with me
like I was someone else,
glancing down my shoulders and hips.
He asked me to sit for him.

Most days I was no one,
the object of his eye
delighting some remnant of lust.
He asked me to undress.

He looked with recognition
at pencils,
sketched the curves of me quickly.
I hid my face in my hair.

13.

His return to canvas coincided with his incapacitation,
his mind smudged and blurred along the outlines
but bright, somehow dynamic
when all else about him was failure.

His thoughts were massive works of architecture
melting into a soft background reality,
helpless and jubilant
in their moment of cohesion and collapse.

His imagination celebratory,
grinding, rough,
he struggled to communicate outside the rectangles of man,
the triangles of overlapping leaves.

His feelings collided on the canvas
and ran through the zigzagging transitions
ineluctably, like lightning seeking ground
and an end.

14.

He was weak.
The studio was cleared and put up for rent.
Light crashed through the windows
looking for him.

He deteriorated
like a tenement in a worthless neighborhood.
I swept the walk
and chased away the kids.

He was finished.
Time travelled forward without him.
He had become a statue
which I worshipped hopelessly.

15.

The small caliber bullet grazed his skull.
The temple's bone doors

shook.
I sat with him until he regained a little consciousness.

I closed his hand around the gun again.
He awoke the strength to lift it,

opened his eyes wide.
In them I saw him walk down the block,

catch a cab, board a plane, look down from the sky.
He showed me the lights of a great city,

took a breath
and blew them into darkness.

THE WORK

BOY WITH A CANDLE

His arm hangs limp at his side.
The black wick still glistens, minutely,
as though he's just blown it out, had done with it.

His other arm sweeps the air before him.
He's looking for something,
groping in a darkness of his own creation.

It's a black hallway, like he's seen in a dream.
Light enters the image from the front, from the viewer,
as though the light of my own body

lit the boy.
I push him ever so gently down the hall.
His gaze is forward, hidden.

We have no need of candles.
The eyes are not the gatherers of light.
His shoulders, in a soft robe, bear the light.

THE FLATIRON BUILDING

On the sidewalk, a man—almost a stick figure,
so small is he,
his body-gesture barely discernible, an elongation—
hails a cab.

The Flatiron Building casts a huge geometrical shadow
across Fifth Avenue,
putting half the city in a crosshatch of anonymity.
The other half is blueprint.

Broadway flows wide around an unpopulated sandbar.
23rd Street is no one's friend.
The little man, caught in the ecstasy of his insignificance,
may never get a cab.

THE ELMS

The leafless treetops are mostly fog
for good reason.

The wet trunks line the walkway irregularly,
like herd animals moving slowly,

the vanishing point an old barn somewhere in the fog
beyond the canvas.

Benches a dark, dirty green
too wet to sit on,

a charcoal figure walks on the charcoal pavement
toward the meeting place of the elms.

He holds his hands behind his back
in a scribbly knot.

He twists around to look at me,
his hair all wet.

THREE PEOPLE AT A BUS STOP

They stand apart from each other
in laced boots,
their heads all swept to one side in the wind,
coat hems flipped up.

All pray to the same leeward god,
above their heads a ridiculous little sign
high on a slim pole:
Bus Stop.

They cannot lift their faces to the deity
who slits their eyes
with wind—that wind which has blown away
all but the signpost.

Their shadows are three spears
vibrating in the wind,
their fists clenched in coat pockets
in bitter prayer.

SUSPENSION BRIDGE

The cables are dissolved in the atmosphere,
in sea-smeared blues, grays, yellows,

fog.
Only the archaic remains:

the roadway, the towers,
and gulls.

The birds are insignificant, two hairline brushstrokes each,
neither coming nor going.

The structure hovers in the mist.
He who consummates his life on the bridge

leaps into God's mind.
In the terrible, cold air,

even the gulls are silent.

BIRD CAGE

Behind the Victorian complexity of the cage,
the open window represents the obvious
and the brick wall across the alley
the next world.

The bird is a cloud of yellow feathers
perched on a swing,
head thrown back, beak wide open,
singing at the top of its lungs,

or screaming.
The curtains, diaphanous white, blow outward
seductively.
The cage door is open.

The bird clings insanely to its perch.
Its stiff red legs and scaly claws
contain its entire intelligence,
the beating wings a yellow blur.

SEATED WOMAN

Sitting upright in a straight chair,
as she insisted,
hands on spread knees, like a judge,
she breathes uncomfortably.

Her lapels drip down her white breasts
like chocolate on ice cream.
Her lap is a pool of hot and cold black.
Her black slacks fall like shadows to the floor.

Her feet are bare—at home, after work,
the toes curling badly.
Every detail of her face is rendered faithfully,
her glare suspicious, the eyes glinting with agony.

STREET VENDOR

His table is fitted with bicycle wheels—for a fast getaway.
He stands at ease, head turned fully to one side,
always looking half a block down the street.
I have inked his eye to hold it open.

The background is a wallpaper of brown brick and opaque
            windows.
Cutouts of two yellow cabs fill the foreground with intensity.
Among the snow globes crowded on the jiggling cart,
one with a street scene: a cab, a brick wall,

and between them on the pavement a small body
with a dot of red paint on its chest,
drifts of still snow.
Above the vendor, T-shirts hang like martyrs on a hill.

A Barbarian at the Gate

As I remember him—black suit, red tie,
a bit devilish,

he stands at the bar, one leg cocked,
one eyebrow cocked.

He contemplates a few coins in his cupped hand,
brooding like a dark philosopher.

The money glows in the light of his palm,
fooling him.

His evening at an end,
the invisible object of his thought

eludes him.
A cigarette burns in the ashtray,

his beer glass empty,
a residue of foam sliding down from the rim.

He is a lovely drunk,
eloquent and sure-footed in his stupor.

TRIPTYCH

1.

The bald bartender,
an old house without trees,
leans against the backbar, settled comfortably.

2.

He smiles for a new arrival,
his teeth, the ruined walls of a country church,
his salute soldierly.

3.

Holding four enormous beer mugs in each hand
like blazing pistons,
he spits fire and smoke joyously.

SELF-PORTRAIT

Covered in diamonds and bells,
I am a harlequin—

seated on the kitchen table,
legs dangling like Christmas stockings.

I am surrounded by a scattering of pink rose petals
like a great prize.

My face, grease-painted rosy white,
studies itself intently,

the bloody lips
firm.

THE SHEEP MEADOW

A child's yellow sun hangs in a white sky.
The rest is green.

The people resemble numbers, symbols, letters of the alphabet
in the solid colors of preschool toys.

Like refrigerator magnets spread out indecipherably,
they play or sleep.

I have permitted a long yellow drip to dangle from the sun
but not to touch the lawn.

The light is a gift.
I walk among the bodies in the dry summer grass.

NUCLEAR GENERATING STATION

The cooling towers float on tall grass like spaceships
in a misty sunrise of their own making.
A barge moves warily on the river.

On the far shore
a commuter train stretches all the way back to Connecticut,
the executive's equipage chased by blackbirds.

His tyranny is overthrown
not by conspirators with knives in their quaking hands
but in a garbage strike, a blackout.

So the tyranny of consciousness is overthrown,
the mind quivering in a gas chamber
of its own design.

VERDI SQUARE

Protesters have chalked the outlines of their bodies.
The figures link arms and dance.

The body is hollow,
our joy silent.

A street performer's mouth is open in song,
his guitar case a stomach.

Verdi looks down from his pedestal
upon children

whom he does not understand
or acknowledge

except to look down on them.
In April, daffodils surround the old man,

and he might as well be dead.

EVENING LIGHTS OF A GREAT CITY

On the museum roof,
she holds a glass of wine with both hands.
Across the lamp-dotted park, the lights of the city blossom.
She is beautiful.

I can't paint what I mean.
I give her a long dress, blue-black in the night,
her shoulders bare, lit from within,
a lavish lantern burning low.

Her face is always turned toward me,
her look
complex, honest—a hint of wetness on her lips,
a question.

This is my answer.
A few faint stars hold out, nestled in the smoky firmament.
I lift my glass to her, dab a reflection in each eye,
and paint no more.

About the Author

Richard Carr grew up in Blue Earth, Minnesota, and now lives in Minneapolis.

His writing has appeared in *Poetry East*, *Exquisite Corpse*, *New Letters*, *Painted Bride Quarterly* and many other journals.

His chapbooks include *Our Blue Earth* (Texas Review Press), *Butterfly and Nothingness* (a poetry hypertext published by Mudlark) and *Letters from North Prospect* (winner of the Frank Cat Press Poetry Chapbook Award).

His full-length poetry collections are *Fitzpatrick* (Broadstone Books), *Grave Reading* (Unsolicited Press), *Lucifer* (Logan House Press), *Dead Wendy* (FutureCycle Press), *Imperfect Prayers* (Steel Toe Books), *One Sleeve* (Evening Street Press), *Ace* (Word Works Books), *Honey* (Gival Press), *Street Portraits* (Backwaters Press), and *Mister Martini* (University of North Texas Press).

His honors include the Holland Prize for *Lucifer*, the FutureCycle Poetry Prize for *Dead Wendy*, the Washington Prize for *Ace*, the Gival Press Poetry Award for *Honey*, and the Vassar Miller Prize for *Mister Martini*.